ENJOYING
A RICH AND
FULFILLING LIFE

EDITED BY
RICHARD SHEA

RUTLEDGE HILL PRESS®
NASHVILLE, TENNESSEE
A THOMAS NELSON COMPANY

Published by Rutledge Hill Press, a Thomas Nelson Company, P.O. Box 141000, Nashville, Tennessee 37214.

This book is an abridged version of *The Book of Success*, edited by Richard Shea, published in 1993 by Rutledge Hill Press.

ISBN 1-55853-898-4

Printed in Colombia
1 2 3 4 5 6 7 8 9—05 04 03 02 01

Contents

PREFACE

During twenty-five years as a professional speechwriter, I collected the better thoughts and observations from some of our wisest thinkers and writers. What began as an exercise to enhance my writing later turned into a habit, and then into a hobby. The result was folders full of pieces of paper all bearing exciting ideas and opinions that I considered too valuable to discard. All of these phrases had something in common. More than a conglomeration of mere words, the quotes that affected me most had contributed to my quest for success—as a professional and as a person.

In the following pages I have collected these ideas into categories that touch on all phases of successful living.

I realize there is no single formula for a happy life or for success, and that success, like happiness, is often elusive when we pursue it as an end in itself. I suspect, however, that while reading the following pages, many of you will find yourselves suddenly looking up and exclaiming, "That idea is just what I've been looking for! Perfect!"

Enjoying a Rich and Successful Life is intended as a handy and regular companion. What attracted me to these quotations in the first place is the accumulated wisdom they represent. They are ideas that have guided generations on their way to enjoying rich and fulfilling lives. So refer to it often—regardless of your circumstances—for its purpose is to serve you, the reader, on your road to a successful life.

—Richard Shea

1

YOUTH:
THE BEST YEARS
OF YOUR LIFE,
OR SO THEY SAY

To find the exact answer, one must first ask the exact question.

—S. TOBIN WEBSTER, BRITISH ANGLICAN CLERGYMAN
(1896–1962)

∽

If one advances confidently in the direction of his dreams and endeavors to live the life he imagined, he will meet with a success unexpected in common hours.

—HENRY DAVID THOREAU, AMERICAN PHILOSOPHER
(1817–1862)

∽

During the first period of a man's life, the danger is not to take the risk.

—SÖREN KIERKEGAARD, DANISH PHILOSOPHER (1813–1855)

Danger and delight grow on one stalk.

—SCOTTISH PROVERB

ↄ

Keep away from people who try to belittle your ambitions. Small people always do that, but the really great make you feel that you, too, can become great.

—MARK TWAIN (SAMUEL L. CLEMENS),
AMERICAN HUMORIST (1835–1910)

ↄ

Risk! Risk anything! Care no more for the opinion of others, for those voices. Do the hardest thing on earth for you. Act for yourself. Face the truth.

—KATHERINE MANSFIELD, NEW ZEALAND-BORN
BRITISH AUTHOR (1888–1923)

If thou art a man, admire those who attempt great things, even though they fail.

—LUCIUS ANNAEUS SENECA,
ROMAN AUTHOR (4 B.C.–A.D. 65)

∽

Whatever you can do, or dream you can, begin it. Boldness has genius, power, and magic in it.

—JOHANN WOLFGANG VON GOETHE,
GERMAN AUTHOR (1749–1832)

∽

You cannot have a proud and chivalrous spirit if your conduct is mean and paltry; for whatever a man's actions are, such must be his spirit.

—DEMOSTHENES, GREEK ORATOR (385?–322 B.C.)

Why should we be in such desperate haste to succeed, and in such desperate enterprises? If a man does not keep pace with his companions, perhaps it is because he hears a different drummer. Let him step to the music which he hears, however measured and far away. It is not important that he should mature as soon as an apple tree or an oak.

—HENRY DAVID THOREAU, AMERICAN PHILOSOPHER (1817-1862)

It is a great art to saunter.

—HENRY DAVID THOREAU, AMERICAN PHILOSOPHER (1817-1862)

There is the greatest practical benefit in making a few failures early in life.

—THOMAS HENRY HUXLEY, BRITISH ZOOLOGIST (1825-1895)

Courage and perseverance have a magical talisman, before which difficulties disappear and obstacles vanish into air.

—JOHN QUINCY ADAMS, U.S. PRESIDENT (1767–1848)

And above all things, never think that you're not good enough yourself. A man should never think that. My belief is that in life people will take you at your own reckoning.

—ANTHONY TROLLOPE, BRITISH AUTHOR (1815–1882)

The supreme end of education is expert discernment in all things—the power to tell the good from the bad, the genuine from the counterfeit, and to prefer the good and the genuine to the bad and the counterfeit.

—SAMUEL JOHNSON, BRITISH AUTHOR AND LEXICOGRAPHER
(1709–1784)

Whom do I call educated? First, those who manage well the circumstances they encounter day by day. . . . Next, those who are decent and honorable in their intercourse with all men, bearing easily and good naturedly what is offensive in others and being as agreeable and reasonable to their associates as is humanly possible to be . . . those who hold their pleasures always under control and are not ultimately overcome by their misfortunes . . . those who are not spoiled by their successes, who do not desert their true selves but hold their ground steadfastly as wise and sober-minded men.

—SOCRATES, GREEK PHILOSOPHER (470?–399 B.C.)

It is almost the definition of a gentleman to say that he is one who never inflicts pain.

—CARDINAL JOHN HENRY NEWMAN, BRITISH PRELATE
AND THEOLOGIAN (1801–1890)

My candle burns at both ends;
It will not last the night;
But, ah, my foes, and oh, my friends—
It gives a lovely light.

—EDNA ST. VINCENT MILLAY, AMERICAN POET (1892–1950)

⁓

She knew how to trust people . . . a rare quality, revealing a
character far above average.

—CARDINAL JEAN FRANÇOIS DE RETZ, FRENCH POLITICIAN
AND MAN OF LETTERS (1614–1679)

⁓

Politeness is to human nature what warmth is to wax.

—ARTHUR SCHOPENHAUER, GERMAN PHILOSOPHER
(1788–1860)

2

WHAT WILL I WANT TO BE DOING EVERY DAY TEN YEARS FROM NOW?

It is the first of all problems for a man to find out what kind of work he is to do in this universe.
—THOMAS CARLYLE, SCOTTISH AUTHOR (1795–1881)

I am a writer because writing is the thing I do best.
—FLANNERY O'CONNOR, AMERICAN AUTHOR (1925–1964)

The world judge of men by their ability in their professions, and we judge of ourselves by the same test; for it is on that on which our success in life depends.
—WILLIAM HAZLITT, BRITISH ESSAYIST (1778–1830)

The man who is born with a talent which he was meant to use finds his greatest happiness in using it.

—JOHANN WOLFGANG VON GOETHE,
GERMAN AUTHOR (1749–1832)

❧

The test of a vocation is the love of the drudgery it involves.

—LOGAN PEARSALL SMITH,
AMERICAN ESSAYIST (1865–1946)

❧

Anything you're good at contributes to happiness.

—BERTRAND RUSSELL, BRITISH PHILOSOPHER (1872–1970)

When work is a pleasure, life is a joy! When work is duty, life is slavery.

—MAXIM GORKY, RUSSIAN AUTHOR (1868–1936)

We could hardly wait to get up in the morning!

—WILBUR WRIGHT AND ORVILLE WRIGHT,
AMERICAN INVENTORS (1867–1912; 1871–1948)

What is work and what is not work are questions that perplex the wisest of men.

—THE BHAGAVAD-GITA, HINDU HOLY BOOK

If people only knew how hard I work to gain my mastery, it wouldn't seem so wonderful at all.

—MICHELANGELO BUONARROTI, ITALIAN ARTIST (1475–1564)

I never did anything worth doing by accident; nor did any of my inventions come by accident; they came by work.

—THOMAS ALVA EDISON, AMERICAN INVENTOR (1847–1931)

Leisure my be defined as free activity, labor as compulsory activity. Leisure does what it likes, labor does what it must, the compulsion being that of Nature, which in these latitudes leaves men no choice between labor and starvation.

—GEORGE BERNARD SHAW, IRISH-BORN BRITISH
PLAYWRIGHT (1856–1950)

If he [Tom Sawyer] had been a great and wise philosopher, like the writer of this book, he would now have comprehended that Work consists of whatever a body is obliged to do and Play consists of whatever a body is not obliged to do.

—MARK TWAIN (SAMUEL L. CLEMENS),
AMERICAN HUMORIST (1835–1910)

Inspiration comes of working every day.

—CHARLES PIERRE BAUDELAIRE, FRENCH POET (1821–1867)

Lord, grant that I may always desire more than I can accomplish.

—MICHELANGELO BUONARROTI, ITALIAN ARTIST (1475–1564)

They talk of the dignity of work. The dignity is in leisure.

—HERMAN MELVILLE, AMERICAN AUTHOR (1819–1891)

Let us do our duty in our shop or in our kitchen, in the market, the street, the office, the school, the home, just as faithfully as if we stood in the front rank of some great battle, and knew that victory for mankind depends on our bravery, strength, and skill. When we do that, the humblest of us will be serving in that great army which achieves the welfare of the world.

—THEODORE PARKER, AMERICAN CLERGYMAN (1810–1860)

Whatsoever thy hand findeth to do, do it with thy might; for there is no work, or device, nor knowledge, nor wisdom, in the grave whither thou goest.

—ECCLESIASTES

A man is a worker. If he is not, then he is nothing.
—JOSEPH CONRAD, POLISH-BORN
BRITISH AUTHOR (1857–1924)

The precise form of an individual's activity is determined, of course, by the equipment with which he came into the world. In other words, it is determined by his heredity.
—HENRY LOUIS (H. L.) MENCKEN, AMERICAN AUTHOR
(1880–1956)

3

IT'S ALMOST LIKE STANDING ASIDE AND WATCHING YOURSELF IN ACTION

Who in the world am I? Ah, that's the great puzzle.
—LEWIS CARROLL (CHARLES L. DODGSON),
BRITISH MATHEMATICIAN AND AUTHOR (1832–1898)

∽

One must know oneself. If this does not serve to discover
truth, it at least serves as a rule of life and there is nothing better.
—BLAISE PASCAL, FRENCH PHILOSOPHER
AND MATHEMATICIAN (1623–1662)

∽

At bottom every man knows well enough that he is a unique
being, only once on this earth; and by no extraordinary chance
will such a marvelously picturesque piece of diversity in unity
as he is ever be put together a second time.
—FRIEDRICH WILHELM NIETZSCHE, GERMAN PHILOSOPHER
(1844–1900)

A man generally has the good or ill qualities he attributes to mankind.

—WILLIAM SHENSTONE, BRITISH POET (1714–1763)

It is with trifles and when he is off guard that a man best reveals his character.

—ARTHUR SCHOPENHAUER, GERMAN PHILOSOPHER (1788–1860)

I have often thought the best way to define a man's character would be to seek out the particular mental or moral attitude in which, when it came upon him, he felt himself most deeply and intensely active and alive. At such moments there is a voice inside which speaks and says: "This is the real me!"

—WILLIAM JAMES, AMERICAN PSYCHOLOGIST
AND PHILOSOPHER (1842–1910)

Few men are of one plain, decided color; most are mixed, shaded or blended; and vary as much from different situations, as changeable silks do from different lights.

—PHILIP DORMER STANHOPE, EARL OF CHESTERFIELD, ENGLISH STATESMAN AND AUTHOR (1694–1773)

What you do speaks so loud that I cannot hear what you say.

—RALPH WALDO EMERSON, AMERICAN AUTHOR (1803–1882)

A man never describes his own character so clearly as when he describes another.

—JEAN PAUL RICHTER, GERMAN SATIRIST (1763–1825)

People seem not to see that their opinion of the world is also
a confession of character.

— RALPH WALDO EMERSON, AMERICAN AUTHOR (1803–1882)

Know thyself. A maxim as pernicious as it is ugly. Whoever
studies himself arrests his own development. A caterpillar
who seeks to know himself would never become a butterfly.

— ANDRÉ GIDE, FRENCH AUTHOR (1869–1951)

Our works are the mirror wherein the spirit first sees its
natural lineaments. Hence, too, the folly of that impossible
precept, Know thyself; till it be translated into this partially
possible one, Know what thou canst work at.

— THOMAS CARLYLE, SCOTTISH AUTHOR (1795–1881)

The world is a looking glass, and gives back to every man the reflection of his own face.

—William Makepeace Thackeray,
British author (1811–1863)

ৎ

I want, by understanding myself, to understand others. I want to be all that I am capable of becoming. . . . This all sounds very strenuous and serious. But now that I have wrestled with it, it's no longer so. I feel happy—deep down. All is well.

—Katherine Mansfield, New Zealand–born
British author (1888–1923)

ৎ

It was prettily devised of Aesop, "The fly sat on the axle tree of the chariot wheel and said, 'What dust do I raise!'"

—Francis Bacon, English statesman, philosopher,
and essayist (1561–1626)

4

IS EVERYONE ALWAYS TRYING TO IMPROVE THEMSELVES AS I AM?

I know of no more encouraging fact than the unquestioned
ability of a man to elevate his life by conscious endeavor.

—HENRY DAVID THOREAU, AMERICAN PHILOSOPHER
(1817–1862)

∽

For who is pleased with himself?

—SAMUEL JOHNSON, BRITISH AUTHOR AND LEXICOGRAPHER
(1709–1784)

∽

Who is not satisfied with himself will grow; who is not so
sure of his own correctness will learn many things.

—PALESTINIAN MAXIM

Men acquire a particular quality by constantly acting a particular way. . . . We become just by performing just actions, temperate by performing temperate actions, brave by performing brave actions.

—ARISTOTLE, GREEK PHILOSOPHER (384–322 B.C.)

He who asks of life nothing but the improvement of his own nature . . . is less liable than anyone else to miss and waste life.

—GENERAL HENRI FRÉDÉRIC AMIEL, SWISS EDUCATOR
AND PHILOSOPHER (1821–1881)

Human beings, by changing the inner attitudes of their minds, can change the outer aspects of their lives.

—WILLIAM JAMES, AMERICAN PSYCHOLOGIST AND
PHILOSOPHER (1842–1910)

The duty of man is the same in respect to his own nature as in respect to the nature of all other things, namely not to follow it but to amend it.

—JOHN STUART MILL, BRITISH ECONOMIST
AND PHILOSOPHER (1806–1873)

We must always change, renew, rejuvenate ourselves; otherwise we harden.

—JOHANN WOLFGANG VON GOETHE,
GERMAN AUTHOR (1749–1832)

I tell you that as long as I can conceive something better than myself I cannot be easy unless I am striving to bring it into existence or clearing the way for it.

—GEORGE BERNARD SHAW, IRISH-BORN BRITISH PLAYWRIGHT
(1856–1950)

The hell to be endured hereafter, of which theology tells, is no worse than the hell we make for ourselves in this world by habitually fashioning our characters in the wrong way.

—WILLIAM JAMES, AMERICAN PSYCHOLOGIST
AND PHILOSOPHER (1842–1910)

I realized the problem was me and nobody could change me except myself.

—JOHN PETWORTH, BRITISH ESSAYIST (1835–1904)

Long years must pass before the truths we have made for ourselves become our very flesh.

—PAUL AMBROISE VALÉRY, FRENCH POET (1871–1945)

Every action we take, everything we do, is either a victory or defeat in the struggle to become what we want to be.

—ANNE BYRHHE, NORWEGIAN FAMILY COUNSELOR
(1906–1981)

෴

I have discovered that we may be in some degree whatever character we choose. Besides, practice forms a man to anything.

—JAMES BOSWELL, SCOTTISH BIOGRAPHER (1740–1795)

෴

It is enough that we set out to mold the motley stuff of life into some form of our own choosing; when we do, the performance is itself the wage.

—LEARNED HAND, AMERICAN JURIST (1872–1961)

The self is not something ready-made, but something in
continuous formation through choice of action.

—JOHN DEWEY, AMERICAN EDUCATOR
AND PHILOSOPHER (1859–1952)

❧

It is necessary to try to surpass one's self always; this
occupation ought to last as long as life.

—CHRISTINA, SWEDISH QUEEN (1626–1689)

❧

We sow our thoughts, and we reap our actions.
We sow our actions, and we reap our habits.
We sow our habits, and we reap our characters;
We sow our characters, and we reap our destiny.

—ANONYMOUS

Habit, if not resisted, soon becomes necessity.
—SAINT AUGUSTINE, NORTH AFRICAN–BORN CHURCH FATHER
(354–430)

We must make automatic and habitual, as early as possible, as many useful actions as we can . . . in the acquisition of a new habit, we must take care to launch ourselves with as strong and decided initiative as possible. . . . Never suffer an exception to occur till the new habit is securely rooted in your life.
—WILLIAM JAMES, AMERICAN PSYCHOLOGIST
AND PHILOSOPHER (1842–1910)

Character is simply habit long continued.
—PLUTARCH, GREEK BIOGRAPHER AND PHILOSOPHER
(46?–120?)

There is a form of eminence which does not depend on fate; it is an air which sets us apart and seems to portend great things; it is the value which we unconsciously attach to ourselves; it is the quality which wins us deference of others; more than birth, position, or ability, it gives us ascendance.

—FRANÇOIS, DUC DE LA ROCHEFOUCAULD,
FRENCH AUTHOR (1613–1680)

The creation of Cary Grant took more than the accent; it took time and practice on the walk, the talk, and all those other mannerisms. "I pretended to be somebody I wanted to be, and I finally became that person," Mr. Grant said, "or he became me. Or we met at some point. It's a relationship."

—*WASHINGTON POST* OBITUARY OF ACTOR CARY GRANT

The never-ending task of self improvement . . .

—RALPH WALDO EMERSON, AMERICAN AUTHOR (1803–1882)

Withdraw into yourself and look. And if you do not find yourself beautiful yet, act as does the creator of a statue that is to be made beautiful: he cuts away here, he smoothes there, he makes this line lighter, this other purer, until a lovely face has grown upon his work. So do you also: cut away all that is excessive, straighten all that is crooked, bring light to all that is overcast, labor to make all one glow of beauty and never cease chiseling your statue, until there shall shine out on you from it the godlike splendor of virtue, until you see the perfect goodness surely established in the stainless shrine.

—PLOTINUS, EGYPTIAN-BORN ROMAN PHILOSOPHER
(205?–270)

5

What Needs to Be Done That I Don't Want to Do—I Must Do Today

We distinguish the excellent man from the common man by saying that the former is the one who makes great demands on himself, and the latter who makes no demands on himself.

—JOSÉ ORTEGA Y GASSET, SPANISH PHILOSOPHER, AUTHOR, AND POLITICIAN (1883–1955)

I have known many who could not when they would, for they had not done it when they could.

—FRANÇOIS RABELAIS, FRENCH AUTHOR (1494?–1553)

To will is to select a goal, determine a course of action that will bring one to that goal, and then hold to that action till the goal is reached. The key is action.

—MICHAEL HANSON, AMERICAN MATHEMATICIAN (1863–1908)

Whether you find satisfaction in life depends not on your tale of years, but on your will.

—MICHEL EYQUEM DE MONTAIGNE, FRENCH ESSAYIST
(1533–1592)

∽

They can because they think they can.

—VIRGIL (PUBLIUS VERGILIUS MARO), ROMAN POET (70–19 B.C.)

∽

Perhaps the most valuable result of all education is the ability to make yourself do the thing you have to do, when it ought to be done, whether you like it or not; it is the first lesson that ought to be learned; and however early a man's training begins, it is probably the last lesson he learns thoroughly.

—THOMAS HENRY HUXLEY, BRITISH ZOOLOGIST (1825–1895)

We improve ourselves by victories over ourself. There must be contests, and we must win.

—EDWARD GIBBON, BRITISH HISTORIAN (1737–1794)

It is energy—the central element of which is will—that produces the miracle that is enthusiasm in all ages. Everywhere it is what is called force of character and the sustaining power of all great action.

—SAMUEL SMILES, SCOTTISH AUTHOR (1812–1904)

Cheerfulness in most cheerful people is the rich and satisfying result of strenuous discipline.

—EDWIN PERCY WHIPPLE, AMERICAN ESSAYIST (1819–1886)

A man can do all things if he but wills them.

—LEON BATTISTA ALBERTI, ITALIAN ARCHITECT (1404–1472)

Do every day or two something for no other reason than you would rather not do it, so that when the hour of dire need draws nigh, it may find you not unnerved and untrained to stand the test.

—WILLIAM JAMES, AMERICAN PSYCHOLOGIST
AND PHILOSOPHER (1842–1910)

Most powerful is he who has himself in his own power.

—LUCIUS ANNAEUS SENECA, ROMAN AUTHOR (4 B.C.–A.D. 65)

The undertaking of a new action brings new strength.

—EVENIUS, ROMAN WRITER (42 B.C. –A.D. 13)

We never know how high we are
Till we are called to rise.
And then, if we are true to plan,
Our statures touch the skies.

—EMILY DICKINSON, AMERICAN POET (1830–1886)

Who then is free? The wise man who can govern himself.

—HORACE (QUINTUS HORATIUS FLACCUS), ROMAN POET
(65–8 B.C.)

6

THE QUIET
POWER OF COURAGE

If we take the generally accepted definition of bravery as a quality which knows no fear, I have never seen a brave man. All men are frightened. The more intelligent they are, the more they are frightened.

—GENERAL GEORGE S. PATTON, AMERICAN GENERAL
(1885–1945)

✍

What a new face courage puts on everything!

—RALPH WALDO EMERSON, AMERICAN AUTHOR,
(1803–1882)

✍

The bravest thing you can do when you are not brave is to profess courage and act accordingly.

—CORRA HARRIS, AMERICAN WRITER (1869–1935)

Be still my heart; thou hast known worse than this.

—HOMER, GREEK POET (C. 850? B.C.)

∽

Let a man who has to make his fortune in life remember this maxim: Attacking is the only secret. Dare and the world yields, or if it beats you sometimes, dare it again and it will succeed.

—WILLIAM MAKEPEACE THACKERAY, BRITISH AUTHOR
(1811–1863)

∽

Facing it, always facing it, that's the way to get through. Face it.

—JOSEPH CONRAD, POLISH-BORN BRITISH AUTHOR
(1857–1924)

I would define true courage to be a perfect sensibility of the measure of danger, and a mental willingness to endure it.

—GENERAL WILLIAM TECUMSEH SHERMAN,
AMERICAN UNION GENERAL (1820–1891)

A light supper, a good night's sleep, and a fine morning have sometimes made a hero of the same man who, by an indigestion, a restless night, and a rainy morning would have proved a coward.

—PHILIP DORMER STANHOPE, EARL OF CHESTERFIELD,
ENGLISH STATESMAN AND AUTHOR (1694–1773)

You have endured worse things; God will grant an end even to these.

—VIRGIL (PUBLIUS VERGILIUS MARO), ROMAN POET (70–19 B.C.)

Courage stands halfway between cowardice and rashness,
one of which is a lack, the other an excess of courage.

—PLUTARCH, GREEK BIOGRAPHER AND PHILOSOPHER
(46? –120?)

Death was afraid of him because he had the heart of a lion.

—ARAB PROVERB

Courage is doing what you're afraid to do. There can be no
courage unless you are scared.

—EDWARD VERNON (EDDIE) RICKENBACKER, AMERICAN
AVIATOR AND BUSINESSMAN (1890–1973)

49

Take calculated risks. That is quite different from being rash.
—GENERAL GEORGE S. PATTON, AMERICAN GENERAL
(1885–1945)

✍

The desire for safety stands against every great and noble enterprise.
—PUBLIUS CORNELIUS TACITUS, ROMAN HISTORIAN
AND ORATOR (55?–120?)

✍

You gain strength, courage, and confidence by each experience in which you really stop to look fear in the face. You are able to say to yourself, "I have lived through this horror. I can take the next thing that comes along."
—ELEANOR ROOSEVELT, AMERICAN DIPLOMAT, AUTHOR,
FIRST LADY (1884–1962)

Courage is the price life exacts for granting peace.

—AMELIA EARHART, AMERICAN AVIATOR (1897–1937?)

∽

I believe that anyone can conquer fear by doing the things
he fears to do, provided he keeps doing them until he gets
a record of successful experiences behind him.

—ELEANOR ROOSEVELT, AMERICAN DIPLOMAT,
AUTHOR, FIRST LADY (1884–1962)

∽

Believe me! The secret of reaping the greatest fruitfulness
and the greatest enjoyment from life is to live dangerously!

—FRIEDRICH WILHELM NIETZSCHE, GERMAN PHILOSOPHER
(1844–1900)

Prudence operates on life in the same manner as rules of composition; it produces vigilance rather than elevation; rather prevents loss than procures advantage; and often miscarriages, but seldom reaches either power or honor.

—SAMUEL JOHNSON, BRITISH AUTHOR AND LEXICOGRAPHER
(1709–1784)

Shun security.

—THALES OF MILETOS, GREEK PHILOSOPHER
AND MATHEMATICIAN (640?–546 B.C.)

What doesn't kill me only makes me stronger.

—FRIEDRICH WILHELM NIETZSCHE, GERMAN PHILOSOPHER
(1844–1900)

7

You Can Win by Fraud and Deceit, but Evil Leaves an Itch You Can't Scratch

There is one thing alone that stands the brunt of life throughout its length: a quiet conscience.

—EURIPIDES, GREEK DRAMATIST (480?–406 B.C.)

༄

What doth it profit a man if he gains the whole world and loses his own soul?

—JESUS OF NAZARETH

༄

And if your friend does evil to you, say to him, "I forgive you for what you did to me, but how can I forgive you for what you did to yourself?"

—FRIEDRICH WILHELM NIETZSCHE, GERMAN PHILOSOPHER (1844–1900)

Only a life lived in the service to others is worth living.
—Albert Einstein, German-born American physicist
(1879–1955)

∽

Among the attributes of God, although they are all equal,
mercy shines with even more brilliance than justice.
—Miguel de Cervantes Saavedra, Spanish author
(1547–1616)

∽

When I do good, I feel good. When I do bad, I feel bad. And
that's my religion.
—Abraham Lincoln, U.S. president (1809–1865)

Life is unfair.
>   —John F. Kennedy, U.S. president (1917–1963)

∽

One ought to examine himself for a very long time before thinking of condemning others.
>   —Molière (Jean Baptiste Poquelin), French dramatist
>   (1622–1673)

∽

The rule of joy and the law of duty seem to me all one.
>   —Oliver Wendell Holmes, Jr., American jurist
>   (1841–1935)

The ideals that have lighted my way and, time after time,
have given me new courage to face life cheerfully have been
Kindness, Beauty, and Truth.

—Albert Einstein, German-born American physicist
(1879–1955)

∽

It is better to suffer wrong than to do it, and happier to be
sometimes cheated than not to trust.

—Samuel Johnson, British author and lexicographer
(1709–1784)

∽

Every man must get to Heaven his own way.

—Frederick II ("the Great"), king of Prussia
(1712–1786)

Wickedness is always easier than virtue, for it takes the short cut to everything.

—JAMES BOSWELL, SCOTTISH BIOGRAPHER (1740–1795)

❧

He who commits injustice is ever made more wretched than he who suffers it.

—PLATO, GREEK PHILOSOPHER (427?–347 B.C.)

❧

What is morality in any given time or place? It is what a majority then and there happen to like, and immorality is what they dislike.

—ALFRED NORTH WHITEHEAD, BRITISH PHILOSOPHER
(1861–1947)

Let justice be done though the heavens fall.

—ROMAN MAXIM

∾

I expect to pass through life but once. If, therefore, there be any kindness I can show or any good thing I can do to any fellow being, let me do it now and not defer or neglect it, as I shall not pass this way again.

—WILLIAM PENN, ENGLISH QUAKER COLONIZER
IN AMERICA (1644–1718)

∾

Forgive, son; men are men; they needs must err.

—EURIPIDES, GREEK DRAMATIST (480?–406 B.C.)

My own experience and development deepen every day my conviction that our moral progress may be measured by the degree in which we sympathize with individual suffering and individual joy.

—GEORGE ELIOT (MARY ANN EVANS), BRITISH NOVELIST
(1819–1880)

And now abideth faith, hope, and charity, these three, but the greatest of these is charity.

—THE FIRST LETTER OF PAUL TO THE CORINTHIANS

The confidence in another man's virtue is no light evidence of a man's own, and God willingly favors such a confidence.

—MICHEL EYQUEM DE MONTAIGNE, FRENCH ESSAYIST
(1533–1592)

Of all the benefits which virtue confers on us, the contempt
of death is one of the greatest.

—MICHEL EYQUEM DE MONTAIGNE, FRENCH ESSAYIST
(1533–1592)

❧

I shall never permit myself to stoop so low as to hate any
man.

—BOOKER T. WASHINGTON, AMERICAN EDUCATOR
AND AUTHOR (1856–1915)

❧

The action is best that secures the greatest happiness for the
greatest number.

—FRANCIS HUTCHESON, IRISH-BORN SCOTTISH PHILOSOPHER
(1694–1746)

No man is above the law, and no man is below it; nor do we ask any man's permission when we require him to obey it.

—THEODORE ROOSEVELT, U.S. PRESIDENT (1858–1919)

Forgiveness is the scent that the rose leaves on the heel that crushes it.

—ANONYMOUS

Here is a rule to remember in the future, when anything tempts you to be bitter; not, "This is a misfortune" but "To bear this worthily is good fortune."

—MARCUS AURELIUS, ROMAN EMPEROR AND PHILOSOPHER (121–180)

8

IMAGINE WHERE WE'D BE IF WE DIDN'T POSSESS OUR GLORIOUS CURIOSITY

No statement should be believed because it is made by an authority.

—HANS REICHENBACH, GERMAN-BORN AMERICAN
PHILOSOPHER AND EDUCATOR (1891–1953)

Oh how fine it is to know a thing or two!

—MOLIÈRE (JEAN BAPTISTE POQUELIN), FRENCH DRAMATIST
(1622–1673)

Aristotle could have avoided the mistake of thinking that women have fewer teeth than men by the simple device of asking Mrs. Aristotle to open her mouth.

—BERTRAND RUSSELL, BRITISH PHILOSOPHER (1872–1970)

I attribute the little I know to my not having been ashamed
to ask for information, and to my . . . conversing with all
descriptions of men on those topics that form their own
peculiar professions and pursuits.

—JOHN LOCKE, ENGLISH PHILOSOPHER (1632–1704)

I am defeated, and know it, if I meet any human being from
whom I find myself unable to learn anything.

—GEORGE HERBERT PALMER, AMERICAN EDUCATOR (1842–1933)

To generalize is to be an idiot. To particularize is alone the
distinction of merit—general knowledges are those knowledges
that idiots possess.

—WILLIAM BLAKE, BRITISH POET (1757–1827)

The important thing is not to stop questioning. Curiosity has its own reason for existing. . . . Never lose a holy curiosity.
—ALBERT EINSTEIN, GERMAN-BORN AMERICAN PHYSICIST (1877–1955)

❧

The degree of one's emotion varies inversely with one's knowledge of the facts—the less you know the hotter you get.
—BERTRAND RUSSELL, BRITISH PHILOSOPHER (1872–1970)

❧

Knowledge itself is power.
—FRANCIS BACON, ENGLISH STATESMAN, PHILOSOPHER, AND ESSAYIST (1561–1626)

The hunger and thirst for knowledge, the keen delight in the chase, the good humored willingness to admit that the scent was false, the eager desire to get on with the work, the cheerful resolution to go back and begin again, the broad good sense, the unaffected modesty, the imperturbable temper, the gratitude for any little help that was given—all these will remain in my memory though I cannot paint them for others.

—FREDERIC WILLIAM MAITLAND, BRITISH JURIST
AND HISTORIAN (1850–1906)

The growth of wisdom may be gauged exactly by the diminution of ill-temper.

—FRIEDRICH WILHELM NIETZSCHE, GERMAN PHILOSOPHER
(1844–1900)

I went to the woods because I wished to live deliberately, to front only the essential facts of life, and see if I could not learn what it had to teach, and not, when I came to die, discover that I had not lived. I did not wish to live what was not life. . . . I wanted to live so sturdily and so Spartan-like as to put to rout all that was not life . . . to drive life into a corner . . . to know it by experience and be able to give an account of it in my next excursion.

—HENRY DAVID THOREAU, AMERICAN PHILOSOPHER (1817–1862)

Wisdom does not show itself so much in precept as in life— in a firmness of mind and mastery of appetite. It teaches us to do as well as talk; and to make our actions and words all of a color.

—LUCIUS ANNAEUS SENECA, ROMAN AUTHOR (4 B.C.–A.D. 65)

The most manifest sign of wisdom is a continual cheerfulness;
her state is like that in the regions above the moon, always
clear and serene.

—MICHEL EYQUEM DE MONTAIGNE, FRENCH ESSAYIST
(1533–1592)

There is much pleasure to be gained from useless knowledge.

—BERTRAND RUSSELL, BRITISH PHILOSOPHER (1872–1970)

Curiosity . . . endows the people who have it with a
generosity in argument and a serenity in their own mode of
life which springs from their cheerful willingness to let life
take the form it will.

—ALISTAIR COOKE, BRITISH-BORN AMERICAN BROADCASTER
AND AUTHOR (1908–)

The mind never need stop growing. Indeed, one of the few experiences which never pall is the experience of watching one's own mind and how it produces new interests, responds to new stimuli, and develops new thoughts, apparently without effort and almost independently of one's own conscious control.

—GILBERT HIGHET, SCOTTISH-BORN AMERICAN CLASSICIST (1906–1978)

Men on their side must force themselves for a while to lay their notions by and begin to familiarize themselves with facts.

—FRANCIS BACON, ENGLISH STATESMAN, PHILOSOPHER, AND ESSAYIST (1561–1626)

9

THE MINUTE HE OPENED HIS MOUTH, YOU COULD TELL HE READ BOOKS

A man who does not read good books has no advantage over the man who can't read them.

— MARK TWAIN (SAMUEL L. CLEMENS),
AMERICAN HUMORIST (1835–1910)

&

When I get a little money, I buy books; and if any is left, I buy food and clothes.

— DESIDERIUS ERASMUS, DUTCH HUMANIST
AND THEOLOGIAN (1524–1583)

&

To sit alone in the lamplight with a book spread out before you and hold intimate converse with men of unseen generations—such is pleasure beyond compare.

— YOSHIDO KENKO, JAPANESE BUDDHIST PRIEST
AND POET (B. 1283)

I've never known any trouble that an hour's reading didn't assuage.

—CHARLES DE SECONDAT, BARON DE MONTESQUIEU,
FRENCH POLITICAL PHILOSOPHER (1689–1755)

❧

A room without books is a body without a soul.

—MARCUS TULLIUS CICERO, ROMAN STATESMAN
AND ORATOR (106–43 B.C.)

❧

Books are the legacies that a great genius leaves to mankind, which are delivered down from generation to generation as presents to the posterity of those who are yet unborn.

—JOSEPH ADDISON, ENGLISH ESSAYIST (1672–1719)

I cannot live without books.

 —THOMAS JEFFERSON, U.S. PRESIDENT (1743–1826)

Without books the development of civilization would have been impossible. They are the engines of change, windows on the world, "lighthouses" as the poet said "erected in the sea of time." They are companions, teachers, magicians, bankers of the treasures of the mind. Books are humanity in print.

 —BARBARA TUCHMAN, AMERICAN HISTORIAN (1912–1989)

My early and invincible love of reading I would not exchange for all the riches of India.

 —EDWARD GIBBON, BRITISH HISTORIAN (1737–1794)

When I am attacked by gloomy thoughts, nothing helps me
so much as running to my books. They quickly absorb me
and banish the clouds from my mind.

—MICHEL EYQUEM DE MONTAIGNE, FRENCH ESSAYIST
(1533–1592)

ꧏ

The reading of all good books is like a conversation with all
the finest men of past centuries.

—RENÉ DESCARTES, FRENCH MATHEMATICIAN
AND PHILOSOPHER (1596–1650)

ꧏ

People say life is the thing, but I prefer reading.

—LOGAN PEARSALL SMITH, AMERICAN ESSAYIST (1865–1946)

The World of Books
Is the Most Remarkable Creation of Man.
Nothing Else That He Builds Ever Lasts.
Monuments Fall;
Nations Perish;
Civilizations Grow Old and Die Out;
And After an Era of Darkness,
New Races Build Others.
But in the World of Books Are Volumes
That Have Seen This Happen Again and Again
And Yet Live On.
Still Young,
Still As Fresh As the Day They Were Written,
Still Telling Men's Hearts,
Of the Hearts of Men Centuries Dead.

—CLARENCE DAY, AMERICAN AUTHOR (1874–1935)

10

IF YOU TAKE YOUR TIME, THINKING IS FUN

I thought about it all the time.
—SIR ISAAC NEWTON, ENGLISH SCIENTIST (1642–1727),
ON HOW HE DISCOVERED THE LAW OF GRAVITY

Thought is subversive and revolutionary, destructive
and terrible; thought is merciless to privilege, established
institutions, and comfortable habit.
—BERTRAND RUSSELL, BRITISH PHILOSOPHER (1872–1970)

When he thinks about something, he doesn't think about it a
little bit, he thinks about it with all his heart and soul.
—A COLLEAGUE'S DESCRIPTION OF DR. HAROLD UREY
(1893–1981), NUCLEAR PHYSICIST AND LUNAR GEOLOGIST

Thought is great and swift and free, the light of the world, the chief glory of man.

—BERTRAND RUSSELL, BRITISH PHILOSOPHER (1872–1970)

Desire to know why, and how—curiosity, which is a lust of the mind, that a perseverance of delight in the continued and indefatigable generation of knowledge—exceedeth the short vehemence of any carnal pleasure.

—THOMAS HOBBES, ENGLISH PHILOSOPHER (1588–1679)

Mental fight means thinking against the current, not with it. . . . It is our business to puncture gas bags and discover the seeds of truth.

—VIRGINIA WOOLF, BRITISH AUTHOR (1882–1941)

There seemed to be one quality of mind which seemed to be of special and extreme advantage in leading him to make discoveries. It was the power of never letting exceptions go unnoticed.

—FRANCIS DARWIN, ON HIS FATHER, CHARLES DARWIN, BRITISH NATURALIST (1809–1882)

The great tragedy of science—the slaying of a beautiful hypothesis by an ugly fact.

—THOMAS HENRY HUXLEY, BRITISH ZOOLOGIST (1825–1895)

If I have made any valuable discoveries, it has been owing more to patient attention than to any other talent.

—SIR ISAAC NEWTON, ENGLISH SCIENTIST (1642–1727)

The fundamental fact about the Greek was that he had to use his mind. The ancient priests had said, "Thus far and no farther. We set the limits of thought." The Greek said, "All things are to be examined and called into question. There are no limits set on thought."

—EDITH HAMILTON, GERMAN-BORN AMERICAN CLASSICIST (1867–1963)

∽

Genius is eternal patience.

—MICHELANGELO BUONARROTI, ITALIAN ARTIST (1475–1564)

∽

The gods plant reason in mankind, of all good gifts the highest.

—SOPHOCLES, GREEK DRAMATIST (496?–406 B.C.)

The temptation to form premature theories upon insufficient data is the bane of our profession.

—SHERLOCK HOLMES, FICTIONAL CHARACTER BY SIR ARTHUR CONAN DOYLE, BRITISH AUTHOR (1859–1930)

∽

Most of the things we do, we do for no better reason than that our fathers have done them or our neighbors do them, and the same is true of a larger part than what we suspect of what we think.

—OLIVER WENDELL HOLMES, JR., AMERICAN JURIST (1841–1935)

∽

The beginning of wisdom is a definition of terms.

—SOCRATES, GREEK PHILOSOPHER (470?–399 B.C.)

Men are apt to mistake the strength of their feeling for the strength of their argument. The heated mind resents the chill touch and relentless scrutiny of logic.

—WILLIAM EWART GLADSTONE, BRITISH POLITICAL LEADER
(1809–1898)

ᔰ

Every great advance in natural knowledge has involved the absolute rejection of authority.

—THOMAS HENRY HUXLEY, BRITISH ZOOLOGIST (1825–1895)

ᔰ

The minute a phrase becomes current, it becomes an apology for not thinking accurately to the end of the sentence.

—OLIVER WENDELL HOLMES, JR., AMERICAN JURIST
(1841–1935)

Many a man fails to become a great thinker only because his memory is too good.

—FRIEDRICH WILHELM NIETZSCHE, GERMAN PHILOSOPHER
(1844–1900)

∽

If any man wishes to write a clear style, let him first be clear in his thoughts.

—JOHANN WOLFGANG VON GOETHE, GERMAN AUTHOR
(1749–1832)

∽

I lived in solitude in the country and noticed how the monotony of a quiet life stimulates the creative mind.

—ALBERT EINSTEIN, GERMAN-BORN AMERICAN PHYSICIST
(1877–1955)

Men give me credit for some genius. All the genius I have is this: When I have a subject in mind, I study it profoundly. Day and night it is before me. My mind becomes pervaded with it . . . the effort which I have made is what people are pleased to call the fruit of genius. It is the fruit of labor and thought.

—ALEXANDER HAMILTON, AMERICAN STATESMAN,
(1755?–1804)

Familiar things happen, and mankind does not bother about them. It requires a very unusual mind to undertake the analysis of the obvious.

—ALFRED NORTH WHITEHEAD, BRITISH PHILOSOPHER
(1861–1947)

Man is not logical, and his intellectual history is a record of mental reserves and compromises. He hangs on to what he can find of his old beliefs even when he is compelled to surrender their logical basis.

—JOHN DEWEY, AMERICAN PHILOSOPHER AND EDUCATOR (1859–1952)

ॐ

'Tis the mind that makes the body rich.

—WILLIAM SHAKESPEARE, ENGLISH DRAMATIST (1564–1616)

ॐ

I thought so hard I got a headache.

—J. D. COBB, STUDENT, ON WHY HIS PAPER WAS LATE

11

Good Health Brings You Lots of Vigor; And, Boy, Does That Make You Tired!

A sound mind in a sound body is a short but full description
of a happy state in this world.

—JOHN LOCKE, ENGLISH PHILOSOPHER (1632–1704)

Cheerfulness is the best promoter of health and is as friendly
to the mind as to the body.

—JOSEPH ADDISON, ENGLISH ESSAYIST (1672–1719)

I am convinced digestion is the great secret of life.

—REV. SYDNEY SMITH, BRITISH CLERGYMAN
AND AUTHOR (1771–1845)

A merry heart doeth good like a medicine.

—THE BOOK OF PROVERBS

∽

True enjoyment comes from activity of the mind and exercise of the body; the two are ever united.

—BARON ALEXANDER VON HUMBOLDT, GERMAN NATURALIST, AUTHOR, AND STATESMAN (1769–1859)

∽

Why do strong arms fatigue themselves with frivolous dumbbells? To dig a vineyard is worthier exercise for men.

—MARTIAL (MARCUS VALERIUS MARTIALIS), ROMAN EPIGRAMMATIST (C. 40–104)

How do you live a long life?
"Take a two-mile walk every morning before breakfast."
—HARRY S. TRUMAN, U.S. PRESIDENT (1884–1972),
ON HIS EIGHTIETH BIRTHDAY

It is impossible to walk rapidly and be unhappy.
—DR. HOWARD MURPHY, AMERICAN PHYSICIAN (1856–1920)

To be free minded and cheerfully disposed at hours of meat and sleep and of exercise is one of the best precepts of long lasting.

—FRANCIS BACON, ENGLISH STATESMAN, PHILOSOPHER,
AND ESSAYIST (1561–1626)

Walking is man's best medicine.

—HIPPOCRATES, GREEK PHYSICIAN (460?–377? B.C.)

༝

What can be added to the happiness of a man who is in health, out of debt, and has a clear conscience?

—ADAM SMITH, SCOTTISH POLITICAL ECONOMIST
AND PHILOSOPHER (1723–1790)

༝

Look to your health; and if you have it, praise God and value it next to conscience; for health is the second blessing that we mortals are capable of, a blessing money cannot buy.

—IZAAK WALTON, ENGLISH ANGLER AND AUTHOR,
(1593–1683)

If you be sick, your own thoughts make you sick.
—BEN JONSON, ENGLISH DRAMATIST (1573–1637)

✍

It is the sign of a dull mind to dwell upon the cares of the body, to prolong exercise, eating and drinking, and other bodily functions. These things are best done by the way; all your attention must be given to the mind.
—EPICTETUS, GREEK STOIC PHILOSOPHER (C. 50–120)

✍

I consider being ill as one of the great pleasures of life, provided one is not too ill.
—SAMUEL BUTLER, BRITISH NOVELIST (1835–1902)

GOOD TALKERS
GO A LONG WAY—
LEARN TO TALK

The reason why so few people are agreeable in conversation is that each is thinking more about what he intends to say than what others are saying.

—FRANÇOIS, DUC DE LA ROCHEFOUCAULD, FRENCH AUTHOR (1613–1680)

Good nature is more agreeable in conversation than wit and gives a certain air to the countenance which is more amiable than beauty.

—JOSEPH ADDISON, ENGLISH ESSAYIST (1672–1719)

Conversation has a kind of charm about it, an insinuating and insidious something that elicits secrets just like love or liquor.

—LUCIUS ANNAEUS SENECA, ROMAN AUTHOR (4 B.C.–A.D. 65)

Speech is civilization itself. The word . . . preserves contact—
it is silence which isolates.

—THOMAS MANN, GERMAN-BORN AMERICAN AUTHOR
(1875–1955)

∽

Gossip and shop talk! That's the fun of a job.

—YOUNG WOMAN ON LUNCH BREAK OVERHEARD
IN A BALTIMORE CAFÉ

∽

In my opinion, the most fruitful and natural play of the mind
is in conversation. I find it sweeter than any other action in
life; and if I were forced to choose, I think I would rather lose
my sight than my hearing and voice. The study of books is a
drowsy and feeble exercise which does not warm you up.

—MICHEL EYQUEM DE MONTAIGNE, FRENCH ESSAYIST
(1533–1592)

The happiest conversation is that of which nothing is distinctly remembered but a general effect of pleasing impression.

—SAMUEL JOHNSON, BRITISH AUTHOR AND LEXICOGRAPHER (1709–1784)

Conversation. What is it? A mystery! It's the art of never seeming bored, of touching everything with interest, of pleasing with trifles, of being fascinating with nothing at all. How do we define this lively darting about with words, of hitting them back and forth, this sort of brief smile of ideas which should be conversation?

—GUY DE MAUPASSANT, FRENCH AUTHOR (1850–1893)

Confidence is courage at ease.

—DANIEL MAHER, AMERICAN PSYCHOLOGIST (1941–)

Never speak of yourself to others; make them talk about themselves instead; therein lies the whole art of pleasing. Everybody knows it, and everyone forgets it.

—EDMOND AND JULES DE GONCOURT, FRENCH AUTHORS
(1822–1896; 1830–1870)

〜

If you can't say anything good about someone, sit right here next to me.

ALICE ROOSEVELT LONGWORTH, AMERICAN SOCIALITE
AND WIT (1884–1980)

〜

Every man becomes, to a certain degree, what the people he generally converses with are.

—PHILIP DORMER STANHOPE, EARL OF CHESTERFIELD,
ENGLISH STATESMAN AND AUTHOR (1694–1773)

Conversation would be vastly improved by the constant use of four simple words: I do not know.

—ANDRÉ MAUROIS, FRENCH AUTHOR (1885–1967)

Listening well and answering well is one of the greatest perfections that can be obtained in conversation.

—FRANÇOIS, DUC DE LA ROCHEFOUCAULD, FRENCH AUTHOR (1613–1680)

There is one topic peremptorily forbidden to all well-bred, to all rational mortals, namely, their distempers. If you have not slept, or if you have slept, or if you have a headache, or sciatica, or leprosy, or thunderstoke, I beseech you, by all the angels, to hold your peace and not pollute the morning.

—RALPH WALDO EMERSON, AMERICAN AUTHOR (1803–1882)

13

A Good Laugh
Is Sunshine
in the House

He has achieved success who has lived well, laughed often, and loved much.

—BESSIE STANLEY, CONTEMPORARY AMERICAN COUNSELOR

Blessed is he who makes his companions laugh.

—THE KORAN

The most wasted of all days is that on which one has not laughed.

—SÉBASTIEN-ROCHE NICOLAS CHAMFORT, FRENCH AUTHOR
(1741–1794)

A good laugh is sunshine in the house.
—WILLIAM MAKEPEACE THACKERAY, BRITISH AUTHOR
(1811–1863)

∾

I am sure that since I have had the full use of my reason,
nobody has heard me laugh.
—PHILIP DORMER STANHOPE, EARL OF CHESTERFIELD,
ENGLISH STATESMAN AND AUTHOR (1694–1773)

∾

No man who has once heartily and wholly laughed can be
altogether irreclaimably bad.
—THOMAS CARLYLE, SCOTTISH HISTORIAN (1795–1881)

The two best physicians of them all—Dr. Laughter
and Dr. Sleep.

—GREGORY DEAN, JR., BRITISH PHYSICIAN (1907–1979)

I quickly laugh at everything for fear of having to cry.

—PIERRE AUGUSTIN CARON DE BEAUMARCHAIS,
FRENCH AUTHOR (1732–1799)

If you like a man's laugh before you know anything of him,
you may say with confidence that he is a good man.

—FEODOR DOSTOYEVSKY, RUSSIAN AUTHOR (1821–1881)

14

LET US
SWEAR
ETERNAL
FRIENDSHIP

Have friends. 'Tis a second existence.
—BALTASAR GRACIÁN, SPANISH PHILOSOPHER (1601–1658)

The mind is so rarely disturbed, but that the company of
a friend will restore it to some degree of tranquility and
sedateness.
—ADAM SMITH, SCOTTISH POLITICAL ECONOMIST
(1723–1790)

When friendship disappears then there is a space left open
to that awful loneliness of the outside world which is like
the cold space between the planets. It is an air in which men
perish utterly.
—HILAIRE BELLOC, FRENCH-BORN BRITISH AUTHOR
(1870–1953)

Madam, I have been looking for a person who dislikes gravy all my life: let us swear eternal friendship.

—REV. SYDNEY SMITH, BRITISH CLERGYMAN AND ESSAYIST
(1771–1845)

Business, you know, may bring you money, but friendship hardly ever does.

—JANE AUSTEN, BRITISH AUTHOR (1775–1817)

Consult your friend on all things, especially on those which respect yourself. His counsel may then be useful where your own self-love might impair your judgment.

—LUCIUS ANNAEUS SENECA, ROMAN AUTHOR (4 B.C.–A.D. 65)

Friendship is almost always the union of a part of one mind with part of another; people are friends in spots.

—GEORGE SANTAYANA, SPANISH-BORN AMERICAN EDUCATOR
AND PHILOSOPHER (1863–1952)

Have no friends not equal to yourself.

—CONFUCIUS, CHINESE PHILOSOPHER (551–479 B.C.)

I desire to so conduct the affairs of this administration that if at the end, when I come to lay down the reins of power, I have lost every other friend on earth, I shall at least have one friend left, and that friend shall be down inside of me.

—ABRAHAM LINCOLN, U.S. PRESIDENT (1809–1865)

So long as we love we serve; so long as we are loved by others, I would almost say we are indispensable; and no man is useless while he has a friend.

—ROBERT LOUIS STEVENSON, SCOTTISH AUTHOR (1850–1894)

Who does not in some sort live to others, does not live much to himself.

—MICHEL EYQUEM DE MONTAIGNE, FRENCH ESSAYIST
(1533–1592)

If a man does not make new acquaintances as he advances through life, he will soon find himself alone. A man, Sir, should keep his friendship in constant repair.

—SAMUEL JOHNSON, BRITISH AUTHOR AND LEXICOGRAPHER
(1709–1784)

I look upon every day to be lost in which I do not make a new acquaintance.

—Samuel Johnson, British author and lexicographer
(1709–1784)

Do not choose for your friends and familiar acquaintances those that are of an estate or quality too much above yours. . . . You will hereby accustom yourselves to live after their rate in clothes, in habit, and in expenses, whereby you will learn a fashion and rank of life above your degree and estate, which will in the end be your undoing.

—Matthew Hale, English jurist (1609–1676)

15

HAPPINESS IS
A BY-PRODUCT

The mind is its own place, and in itself
Can make heav'n of hell, a hell of heaven.

—JOHN MILTON, ENGLISH POET (1608–1674)

A day spent without the sight or sound of beauty, the
contemplation of mystery, or the search of truth or perfection
is a poverty-stricken day; and a succession of such days is
fatal to human life.

—LEWIS MUMFORD, AMERICAN AUTHOR AND CRITIC
(1895–1990)

Happiness is a by-product.

—ROBERT TRANY, AMERICAN WRITER (1928–)

Many who seem to be struggling with adversity are happy; many, amid great affluence, are utterly miserable.
—PUBLIUS CORNELIUS TACITUS, ROMAN HISTORIAN
AND ORATOR (55?–120?)

∽

To live happily is an inward power of the soul.
—MARCUS AURELIUS, ROMAN EMPEROR AND PHILOSOPHER
(121–180)

∽

The mind is master over every kind of fortune; itself acts in both ways, being the cause of its own happiness and misery.
—LUCIUS ANNAEUS SENECA, ROMAN AUTHOR (4 B.C.–A.D. 65)

Human felicity is produced not as much by great pieces of good fortune that seldom happen as by little advantages that occur every day.

—BENJAMIN FRANKLIN, AMERICAN STATESMAN AND AUTHOR
(1706–1790)

ॐ

We must interpret a bad temper as a sign of inferiority.

—ALFRED ADLER, AUSTRIAN PSYCHIATRIST (1870–1937)

ॐ

Happiness is not best achieved by those who seek it directly.

—BERTRAND RUSSELL, BRITISH PHILOSOPHER (1872–1970)

The goal towards which the pleasure principle impels us—of becoming happy—is not attainable; yet we may not—nay, cannot—give up the effort to come nearer to realization of it by some means or other.

—SIGMUND FREUD, AUSTRIAN PSYCHIATRIST (1856–1939)

There is only one way to happiness, and that is to cease worrying about things which are beyond the power of our will.

—EPICTETUS, GREEK STOIC PHILOSOPHER (C. 50–120)

My hopes are not always realized, but I always hope.

—OVID (PUBLIUS OVIDIUS NASO), ROMAN POET
(43 B.C.–A.D. 18)

We are long before we are convinced that happiness is never to be found; and each believes it possessed by others, to keep alive the hope of obtaining it for himself.
—SAMUEL JOHNSON, BRITISH AUTHOR AND LEXICOGRAPHER (1709–1784)

～

We French found it and called it *joie de vivre*—the joy of living.
—RENÉE REPOND, FRENCH ACTRESS (1888–1965)

～

My happiness derives from knowing the people I love are happy.
—HOLLY KETCHEL, CONTEMPORARY AMERICAN WRITER

Formula of my happiness: a Yes, a No, a straight line, a goal.
—FRIEDRICH WILHELM NIETZSCHE, GERMAN PHILOSOPHER
(1844–1900)

၅

Hope is itself a species of happiness, and perhaps the chief
happiness which this world affords.
—SAMUEL JOHNSON, BRITISH AUTHOR AND LEXICOGRAPHER
(1709–1784)

၅

If you are distressed by anything external, the pain is not due
to the thing itself, but to your estimate of it; and thus you
have the power to revoke it at any minute.
—MARCUS AURELIUS, ROMAN EMPEROR AND PHILOSOPHER
(121–180)

Well-being is attained by little and little, and nevertheless is no little thing itself.

—ZENO, GREEK PHILOSOPHER (335–263 B.C.)

❧

How to gain, how to keep, how to recover happiness is in fact for most men at all times the secret motive of all they do, and of all they are willing to endure.

—WILLIAM JAMES, AMERICAN PSYCHOLOGIST
AND PHILOSOPHER (1842–1910)

❧

The happiest people are those who seem to have no particular reason for being happy except that they are so.

—WILLIAM RALPH INGE, BRITISH PRELATE AND THEOLOGIAN
(1860–1964)

16

THE FACTS
OF LIFE

God couldn't be everywhere, so he created mothers.

—Jewish proverb

ᔐ

I believe love produces a certain flowering of the whole personality which nothing else can achieve.

—Ivan Sergeevich Turgenev, Russian novelist
(1818–1883)

ᔐ

A desire to be observed, considered, esteemed, praised, beloved, and admired by his fellows is one of the earliest as well as the keenest dispositions discovered in the heart of man.

—John Adams, U.S. president (1735–1826)

A man can be himself only so long as he is alone.
—ARTHUR SCHOPENHAUER, GERMAN PHILOSOPHER
(1788–1860)

Look, when that crowd gets to cheering, when we know
they're with us, when we know they like us, we play better.
A hell of a lot better!
—BILL CARLIN, AMERICAN PROFESSIONAL FOOTBALL PLAYER

I never come back home with the same moral character I
went out with; something or other becomes unsettled where
I had achieved internal peace; some one or other of the things
I had put to flight reappears on the scene.
—LUCIUS ANNAEUS SENECA, ROMAN AUTHOR (4 B.C.–A.D. 65)

How much trouble he avoids who does not look to see what his neighbor says or does or thinks.

— MARCUS AURELIUS, ROMAN EMPEROR AND PHILOSOPHER (121–180)

∽

The achievements which society rewards are won at the cost of diminution of personality.

— CARL GUSTAV JUNG, SWISS PSYCHIATRIST (1875—1961)

∽

When we talk in company we lose our unique tone of voice, and this leads us to make statements which in no way correspond to our real thoughts.

— FRIEDRICH WILHELM NIETZSCHE, GERMAN PHILOSOPHER (1844–1900)

Public opinion is a permeating influence, and it exacts obedience to itself; it requires us to think other men's thoughts, to speak other men's words, to follow other men's habits.

—WALTER BAGEHOT, BRITISH SOCIAL SCIENTIST (1826–1877)

I care not so much what I am in the opinion of others, as what I am in my own; I would be rich of myself and not by borrowing.

—MICHEL EYQUEM DE MONTAIGNE, FRENCH ESSAYIST (1533–1592)

Character is formed in the stormy billows of the world.

—JOHANN WOLFGANG VON GOETHE, GERMAN AUTHOR (1749–1832)

No man lives without jostling and being jostled; in all ways he has to elbow himself through the world, giving and receiving offense.

—THOMAS CARLYLE, SCOTTISH HISTORIAN (1795–1881)

∽

We become actors without realizing it, and actors without wanting to.

—GENERAL HENRI FRÉDÉRIC AMIEL, SWISS EDUCATOR AND PHILOSOPHER (1821–1881)

∽

You don't learn to hold your own in the world by standing on guard, but by attacking and getting well hammered yourself.

—GEORGE BERNARD SHAW, IRISH-BORN BRITISH PLAYWRIGHT (1856–1950)

Fame always brings loneliness. Success is as ice cold and lonely as the North Pole.

—VICKY BAUM, AUSTRIAN-BORN AMERICAN AUTHOR
(1896–1960)

❧

We live thick and are in each other's way, and stumble over one another, and I think we thus lose some respect for one another.

—HENRY DAVID THOREAU, AMERICAN PHILOSOPHER
(1817–1862)

❧

I hate a fellow whom pride, or cowardice, or laziness drives into a corner, and who does nothing when he is there but sit and growl; let him come out as I do, and bark.

—SAMUEL JOHNSON, BRITISH AUTHOR AND LEXICOGRAPHER
(1709–1784)

To act from pure benevolence is not possible for finite human beings. Human benevolence is mingled with vanity, interest, or some other motive.

—SAMUEL JOHNSON, BRITISH AUTHOR AND LEXICOGRAPHER
(1709–1784)

❦

The crowd gives the leader new strength.

—EVENIUS, ROMAN SCHOLAR (42 B.C.–A.D. 13)

❦

It is the nature of ambition to make men liars and cheaters, to hide the truth in their breasts, and show, like jugglers, another thing in their mouths, to cut all friendships and enmities to the measure of their own interests, and to make good countenance without the help of good will.

—SALLUST (GAIUS SALLUSTIUS CRISPUS), ROMAN HISTORIAN
(86–34 B.C.)

17

IT'S THE NICETIES
THAT MAKE
THE DIFFERENCE

Fate gives us the hand, and we play the cards.
—Arthur Schopenhauer, German philosopher
(1788–1860)

ᔀ

Remember this, that very little is needed to make a happy life.
—Marcus Aurelius, Roman emperor and philosopher
(121–180)

ᔀ

Possessions, outward success, publicity, luxury—to me these have always been contemptible. I assume that a simple and unassuming manner of life is best for everyone, best for both the body and the mind.

Albert Einstein, German-born American physicist
(1879–1955)

The main things which seem to me important on their own account, and not merely as a means to other things, are knowledge, art, instinctive happiness, and relations of friendship or affection.

—BERTRAND RUSSELL, BRITISH PHILOSOPHER (1872–1970)

The impression forces itself upon one that men measure by false standards, that everyone seeks power, success, riches for himself, and admires others who attain them, while undervaluing the truly precious things in life.

—SIGMUND FREUD, AUSTRIAN PSYCHIATRIST (1856–1939)

What is the use of running when we are on the wrong road?

—BAVARIAN PROVERB

Look up, laugh loud, talk big, keep the colour in your cheek and the fire in your eye, adorn your person, maintain your health, your beauty and your animal spirits.
—WILLIAM HAZLITT, BRITISH ESSAYIST (1778–1830)

To live lightheartedly but not recklessly; to be gay without being boisterous; to be courageous without being bold; to show trust and cheerful resignation without fatalism—this is the art of living.
—JEAN DE LA FONTAINE, FRENCH FABULIST (1621–1695)

The shoe that fits one person pinches another; there is no recipe for living that suits all cases.
—CARL GUSTAV JUNG, SWISS PSYCHIATRIST (1875–1961)

The root of the matter . . . the thing I mean . . . is love, Christian love, or compassion. If you feel this, you have a motive for existence, a guide for action, a reason for courage, an imperative necessity for intellectual honesty.

— BERTRAND RUSSELL, BRITISH PHILOSOPHER (1872–1970)

∽

Change your thoughts, and you change your world.

— NORMAN VINCENT PEALE, AMERICAN CLERGYMAN
AND AUTHOR (1898–1993)

∽

At the touch of love, everyone becomes a poet.

— PLATO, GREEK PHILOSOPHER (427?–347 B.C.)

This is what you shall do: love the earth, and sun, and animals, despise riches, give alms to every one that asks, stand up for the stupid and crazy, devote your income and labor to others, hate tyrants, argue not concerning God, have patience and indulgence toward the people, take off your hat to nothing known or unknown, or to any man or number of men; go freely with powerful uneducated persons, and with the young, and mothers of families; read these leaves in the open air every season of every year of your life; re-examine all you have been told at school or church, or in any books, and dismiss whatever insults your own soul.

—WALTER (WALT) WHITMAN, AMERICAN POET (1819–1892)

I hold this as a rule of life: Too much of anything is bad.

—TERENCE (PUBLIUS TERENTIUS AFER), ROMAN AUTHOR
(190?–59 B.C.)

My heart, which is so full to overflowing, has often been solaced and refreshed by music when sick and weary.

—MARTIN LUTHER, GERMAN PROTESTANT RELIGIOUS
REFORMER (1483–1546)

ᔐ

We should consider every day lost in which we have not danced at least once.

—FRIEDRICH WILHELM NIETZSCHE, GERMAN PHILOSOPHER
(1844–1900)

ᔐ

Beauty of style and harmony and grace and good rhythm depend on simplicity.

—PLATO, GREEK PHILOSOPHER (427?–347 B.C.)

Exuberance is beauty.

—William Blake, British poet (1757–1827)

Make no little plans; they have no magic to stir men's blood, and probably themselves will not be realized.

—Daniel Hudson Burnham, American architect (1846–1912)

The moment we indulge our affections, the earth is metamorphosed; here is no winter and no night; all tragedies, all ennuis vanish—all duties even.

—Ralph Waldo Emerson, American author (1803–1882)

Few people have ever seriously wished to be exclusively rational. The good life which most desire is a life warmed by passions and touched with that ceremonial grace which is impossible without some affectionate loyalty to traditional forms and ceremonies.

—JOSEPH WOOD KRUTCH, AMERICAN EDUCATOR
AND NATURALIST (1893–1970)

Music, the greatest good that mortals know,
And all of heaven we have below.

—JOSEPH ADDISON, ENGLISH ESSAYIST (1672–1719)

He that is discontented in one place will seldom be content in another.

—AESOP, GREEK FABULIST (C. 550 B.C.)

We deem those happy who from the experience of life have
learned to bear its ills without being overcome by them.
—CARL GUSTAV JUNG, SWISS PSYCHIATRIST (1875–1961)

He who has a why to live can bear almost any how.
—FRIEDRICH WILHELM NIETZSCHE, GERMAN PHILOSOPHER
(1844–1900)

I have no pleasure in any man who despises music. It is
no invention of ours; it is a gift of God. I place it next to
theology. Satan hates music: he knows how it drives the
evil spirit out of us.
—MARTIN LUTHER, GERMAN PROTESTANT RELIGIOUS
REFORMER (1483–1546)

Indolence is a delightful but distressing state; we must be doing something to be happy. Action is no less necessary than thought to the instinctive tendencies of the human frame.

—MOHANDAS KARAMCHAND (MAHATMA) GANDHI,
INDIAN POLITICAL LEADER (1869–1948)

Civilization . . . is a matter of imponderables, of delight in the things of the mind, of love of beauty, of honor, grace, courtesy, delicate feeling. Where imponderables are things of first importance, there is the height of civilization, and, if at the same time, the power of art exists unimpaired, human life has reached a level seldom attained and very seldom surpassed.

—EDITH HAMILTION, GERMAN-BORN AMERICAN CLASSICIST
(1867–1963)

In everything, satiety closely follows the greatest pleasures.
—MARCUS TULLIUS CICERO, ROMAN STATESMAN AND ORATOR
(106–43 B.C.)

I like to walk about among the beautiful things that adorn the world; but private wealth I should decline, or any sort of personal possessions, because they would take away my liberty.
—GEORGE SANTAYANA, SPANISH-BORN AMERICAN EDUCATOR
AND PHILOSOPHER (1863–1952)

We never reflect how pleasant it is to ask for nothing.
—LUCIUS ANNAEUS SENECA, ROMAN AUTHOR
(4 B.C.–A.D. 65)

One word frees us of all the weight and pain of life.
That word is love.

—SOPHOCLES, GREEK DRAMATIST (496?–406 B.C.)

∽

Has a woman who knew she was well-dressed ever caught
a cold?

—FRIEDRICH WILHELM NIETZSCHE, GERMAN PHILOSOPHER
(1844–1900)

∽

One ought, every day at least, to hear a little song, read a
good poem, see a fine picture, and, if it were possible, to
speak a few reasonable words.

—JOHANN WOLFGANG VON GOETHE,
GERMAN AUTHOR (1749–1832)

The ultimate of being successful is the luxury of giving yourself the time to do what you want to do.

—LEONTYNE PRICE, AMERICAN OPERA SOPRANO (1927–)

In this world there are only two tragedies. One is not getting what one wants, and the other is getting it.

—OSCAR WILDE, IRISH-BORN BRITISH AUTHOR (1854–1900)

What a wonderful life I've had! I only wish I'd realized it sooner!

—COLETTE (SIDONIE GABRIELLE COLETTE), FRENCH NOVELIST (1873–1954)

18

A Reminder

This also—that I live, I consider a gift of God.

—OVID (PUBLIUS OVIDIUS NASO), ROMAN POET
(43 B.C.–A.D. 18)

∽

Death twitches my ear. "Live," he says, "I am coming."

—VIRGIL (PUBLIUS VERGILIUS MARO),
ROMAN POET (70–19 B.C.)

∽

Our lives as we lead them are passed on to others, whether in
physical or mental forms, tingeing all future lives together.
This should be enough for one who lives for truth and service
to his fellow passengers on the way.

—LUTHER BURBANK, AMERICAN HORTICULTURIST
(1849–1926)

The short bloom of our brief and narrow life flies fast away.
While we are calling for flowers and wine and women, old
age is upon us.

—JUVENAL (DECIMUS JUNIUS JUVENALIS), ROMAN SATIRIST
(60?-140?)

∽

I came to the place of my birth and cried, "The friends of my
youth, where are they?" And echo answered, "Where are they?"

ARAB PROVERB

∽

Like Confucius of old, I am so absorbed in the wonder of the
earth and the life upon it, that I cannot think of heaven and
angels.

—PEARL S. BUCK, AMERICAN AUTHOR (1892-1973)

Our dead brothers still live for us and bid us think of life, not death—of life to which in their youth they lent the passion and glory of Spring. As I listen, the great chorus of life and joy begins again, and amid the awful orchestra of seen and unseen powers and destinies of good and evil, our trumpets sound once more a note of daring, hope, and will.
—OLIVER WENDELL HOLMES, JR., AMERICAN JURIST (1841–1935), MEMORIAL DAY ADDRESS 1884

If there is a sin against life, it consists . . . in hoping for another life and in eluding the implacable grandeur of this life.
—ALBERT CAMUS, FRENCH AUTHOR (1913–1960)

*In the final act of the play, Our Town, Emily, a young mother, has
died and gone to Heaven. In the following scene, she has received permission to go back to earth for one day where, alone and unseen by the
earthlings, she can once again be with her family and friends. The
experience unnerves her. The dialogue comes at the end of her brief
stay on earth.*

Emily:
I can't. I can't go on. It goes so fast. We don't have time
to look at one another. (She breaks down sobbing.) I didn't
realize. So all that was going on and we never noticed. Take
me back—up the hill—to my grave. But first, wait! One
more look.

Good-by; good-by, world; good-by, Grover's Corners . . .
Mama and Papa. Good-by to clocks ticking . . . and Mama's
sunflowers. And food and coffee. And new-ironed dresses
and hot baths . . . and sleeping and waking up. Oh, earth,
you're too wonderful for anybody to realize you. (She looks

toward the stage manager and asks abruptly through her tears.) Do any human beings ever realize life while they live it?—every, every minute?

Stage Manager:
No. (Pause) The saints and poets, maybe—they do some.

Emily:
I'm ready to go back.

—THORNTON WILDER, AMERICAN PLAYWRIGHT (1897–1975),

OUR TOWN